Parables contain g
Jesus used them ot.....
fully drawn valuable truths from the drama of
Shark Tank to illustrate self-evident life principles.
His analogy of the secular and the sacred accents
our opportunity and responsibility to insure our
eternal acceptance. The map for that acceptance
and ensuing benefits is carefully drawn.

—DAVE HARDY, DMIN
DALLAS THEOLOGICAL SEMINARY

We all desire to be successful, but in order to suc-
ceed in both business and in life, we need to know
how to navigate where we are or what we have, in
order to obtain the best deal. William Hatfield has
given us the secret to closing the best deal of our
lives.

—MATT MOORE
PRESIDENT, YOUNG BUSINESSMEN OF TULSA
OWNER, HEARTLAND DIRECT INTERNATIONAL

Bill Hatfield's book shows us that a business shark's
deal is profitable to him. The deal Jesus offers us is
always to our benefit. Accepting Christ is the best
offer we could ever get. We are the winners! Peace,
joy, happiness, and eternal life are ours.

—TED ROBERTSON
FOUNDER, ROBERTSON TIRE COMPANY
PRESIDENT, INTERNATIONAL FELLOWSHIP OF
CHRISTIAN BUSINESSMEN

THE
SHARK
TANK
THEOLOGY

WILLIAM KEITH HATFIELD

CREATION
HOUSE

THE SHARK TANK THEOLOGY by William K. Hatfield
Published by Creation House
A Charisma Media Company
600 Rinehart Road
Lake Mary, Florida 32746
www.charismahouse.com

Unless otherwise noted, all Scripture quotations are taken from the King James Version of the Bible.

Cover design by Rachel Lopez
Design Director: Justin Evans

Visit the author's website at www.charitybaptistchurchtulsa. com.

Library of Congress Cataloging-in-Publication Data:
2016938855
An application to register this book for cataloging has been submitted to the Library of Congress.
International Standard Book Number: 978-1-62998-550-3
E-book ISBN: 978-1-62998-551-0

First edition

16 17 18 19 20 — 987654321
Printed in Canada

*I dedicate this book to my beloved wife, Sharon,
my life's companion, best friend,
and greatest inspiration.*

CONTENTS

INTRODUCTION

SHARK TANK HAS become one of the most successful shows on American television. It is based on a Japanese program *Dragons' Den*. Now in its sixth season, *Shark Tank* has become so successful that it is not unusual to see on some stations a *Shark Tank* marathon with episodes running either back-to-back or night after night. A successful spinoff, *After the Tank*, followed in 2015.

The show opens with sharks swimming in a tank like what you might see at an aquarium, set to ominous music, reminiscent of the *Jaws* theme. Then, down a long corridor lined with aquariums, walks one or more people. These are the contestants. They come with a business proposal and a company to pitch to the investors, known as "the Sharks."

As the camera follows their walk toward two massive doors that open into the Shark's room, we are given our first glimpses of the Sharks. There are five of them, sitting in a row, waiting for the entrance of their potential partner (or partners) or victims.

The Sharks are advertised to be self-made millionaires and billionaires. On a rotating basis we see Kevin O'Leary, who became a billionaire after selling the Learning Company; Robert Herjavec, who sold some companies for $350 million; Daymond John, the millionaire founder of the clothing line FUBU; Barbara Corcoran, millionaire real estate investor; Mark Cuban, tech billionaire and owner of the Dallas Mavericks; Lori Greiner of QVC, among other things; and Kevin Harrington, worth $450 million as founder and CEO of several companies, including the Home Shopping Network. Comedian Jeff Foxworthy also makes an occasional appearance. These are the Sharks.

As the contestants arrive at the entrance to the Tank the doors swing open. The facial expressions of the Sharks are shown as they get their first look at the pitchmen. There may already be a display or visual aid set up in their tank, but this is the first time they see who is behind the product. There are smiles when children are included, laughs for funny costumes or when the pitch begins with a humorous element such as masks, gymnastics, or costumes. A memorized spiel follows by the hopeful entrepreneur, one usually very well prepared. It begins with what the pitchman hopes to get from one or more Sharks. It ends with an invitation, sometimes formed as a question such as, "Who wants to partner with me in this fantastic business?"

It is usually pretty quick—the pitch, the questions, and the acceptance or rejection. The contestants may be derided, insulted, humiliated, and reduced to speechlessness or even tears. The Sharks may be angry, petulant, accusatory, or just downright insulting. These "filthy rich" (the show describes them as such) people may often illustrate well why Jesus was so pessimistic about their chances of entering the kingdom of heaven! They may also stoke even higher the fires of resentment many people already have against wealthy people. But often, they will show some compassionate concern and care as they invest in someone because they "believe" in the person, or because they want to help the entrepreneur as they are someone who has worked hard with a lot stacked against them. Some such episode scenes have scored big on YouTube. (See "the farmer pitch" on YouTube.)

The show is examined from every angle, as it is about life, life's lessons, and so much more. It is no wonder that a Google search will turn up all manner of articles regarding its psychology or lessons that can be learned. Episodes are dissected, success stories are put under the microscope, and the best and worst deals are examined by business magazines and newspapers such as *Forbes* and *Wall Street Journal.*

That is what I am doing. I am weighing in. This show provides too good of an opportunity to pass up. It presents an obvious religious application or spiritual connection. It's no wonder that it is such an appealing show and that it has resonated with so many. Its popularity shows no signs of waning. People keep inviting it into their homes each night because it is compelling in it's themes of absolutes, grace, penalty, and punishment. All of these beg for an expression for us who will live for all eternity, as C. S. Lewis put it, "everlasting splendors or eternal horrors." I'm not surprised that the producer of the show, Mark Burnett, is devout Christian. He and his wife, Roma Downey, are famous for producing *The Bible* and *A.D.*, the two series that ran during the 2015 and 2016 Easter seasons.

So I trust you will enjoy these eternal life's lessons from *Shark Tank*.

CHAPTER 1

YOUR ENTRANCE INTO THE TANK

JUST BEGAN WATCHING *Shark Tank* recently. I had changed my satellite subscription to get rid of most of the movies and fiction. I now major on news, sports, documentaries, history, and real shows about real people. While browsing through the offerings, I came upon *Shark Tank* and remembered seeing some promos featuring Mark Cuban. His Mavericks were the favorite NBA team here in Tulsa for many years. That was before Oklahoma City got the Thunder!

Anyway, I TiVoed an episode and watched it later that week. I was just getting used to the new remote and inadvertently set it to tape the series, rather than just one episode. So my queue was full of some of the seven years of episodes by the time I checked it.

I loved it! I watched several episodes in a row, skipping the commercials. The five Sharks' personalities, their tendencies, their quirks, likes, and dislikes, all became clearer then, and over the ensuing weeks. I was hooked!

As a pastor I am often called upon to be a life skills coach. I have lunch with leading businessmen in my community every week. I am a student of life and of the Bible. My library is full of books that challenge me to engage people meaningfully. Everyone we meet is an eternal being. They are important and of great value, so much so that Jesus loved them and died for them. So as I watched *Shark Tank*, I began to see the metaphorical value of it. I saw a lot of basic, primary applications in the process. I began to see how the show presented questions and values that are parallel to those in our lives every day, and to life itself.

So, that was my introduction to the Tank, my entrance into the world of dreamers making pitches in order to gain money and partnerships, all done on national television before a huge viewing audience. On the show, it is a big deal to make an entrance. It means that out of hundreds of thousands of contestants, you somehow made the cut. You were screened heavily. It was decided by the higher-ups that your story was worth telling. Your business was worth the exposure. You had some entertainment value. You were deemed worthy of the opportunity. And with some, you might even gain the rare privilege of being interviewed, showing you at home and in your community, doing what you do. These clips will show before your entrance on the show and will give viewers an opportunity to get acquainted with you and to connect with you emotionally.

Kevin O'Leary likes to point out to the chosen ones how fortunate they are. He will say to one who is at a loss for words or who cannot remember his carefully memorized lines, something like, "That's OK! This is only the biggest moment of your life. This is only as big as it gets!" Smiling and sarcastic, he casts the moment as one with such ramifications that the person's destiny will be greatly impacted by his performance. We sometimes see in the clips that the lives of most who appear on *Shark Tank* are changed significantly, whether they get a deal or not. Television has that kind of power.

So, as you can imagine, a lot of effort goes into making a good impression in that entrance. What to wear, how to walk, whether to look at the cameras in the hallway, and then going through the great doors as they open, with dignity and confidence is carefully thought out and rehearsed. You memorize what you are going to say. You get people to help you with possible questions. The really good contestants watch the previous shows over and over and prepare answers to the difficult questions. Finally, you arrive and the massive doors swing open. You walk forward and position yourself properly on the Persian rug and face the five Sharks with a smile. At some point, the music stops and the signal is given. You make your pitch.

Someday your entrance into the next life will be the most important entrance you ever make. Your presentation *will be* the most important moment of your existence. As you pass from this life into eternity, you will not be going before five judges. You will stand before only One. The Bible tells us that "it is appointed unto man once to die but after this the judgment" (Heb. 9:27).

We are all walking through the long corridor right now to the large doors that will swing open at the end of life. We had better be ready.

Unfortunately, as on the show, many will not be prepared. The Sharks cut many an entrepreneur down, citing lack of numbers, poor presentation, lousy sales, bad ideas, and concepts or products that will never fly. The same is true as we pass. The Bible tells us that "there is a way that seemeth right unto a man, but the end thereof are the ways of death" (Prov. 14:12). Jesus said there are two paths: one narrow and one broad. The broad way has a wide gate and leads to destruction. Many go that way. The narrow way with the straight gate leads to life. (Matt. 7:13–14.) If we enter eternity based on what seems right to us, and are on the wrong path, we lose our one and only chance at salvation.

The masses of people try to live lives that will pass the judgment and meet whatever they understood God's standard to be. Most people try to live and let live. They try to find a formula that will bring peace to their souls and that which makes logical sense to be enough for any just God. This is unfortunate because, like my original computations, they will be way off the mark. I thought I was an astute enough and an educated person to know how a person would fare on the show. I was wrong most of the time because I did not know the rules, principles, and absolutes the judges would use to base their decisions on. So it will be with those who try to please Almighty God with their good works, kindness, and well-lived lives.

Do you know the rules, principles, and absolutes of the most important Judge you will ever deal with? When you go through the doors, will you get a deal? Will He want to partner with you in presence, love, and relationship for all eternity? Or will you get the torment of eternal separation?

Let's be clear on this. The Bible says there is no presentation slick enough to get you the biggest deal of your life, that being eternal salvation. There is no business (or life) model that will earn God's favor. You will never do enough. You will never have enough profit, you will never perfect a business plan, or get enough interest from the big box stores. You will never "impress" your way to a deal with God! His Word on the matter is clear: "Not by works of righteousness which we have done but by His mercy He saved us..." (Titus 3:5). Ephesians 2:8–9 says, "For by grace are ye saved through faith; and that not of yourselves. It is the gift of God: Not of works, lest any man should boast."

You see, I have great news. Unlike *Shark Tank*, you can know when you finish your walk, when you have made your entrance, and when the doors swing open, you already have a deal with the *only* Shark in the tank!

Imagine that! What if you went to Lori or Robert *before* the show and made a deal? When you go into the Tank, *your* presentation does not matter. You already have a deal. *Your* numbers and sales do not matter. You already have a deal. *Your* lack of anything does not matter. Make them mad if you want to. You already have a deal. In fact, you can wear flip-flops, a T-shirt, and cut-offs. It would not matter. You already have a deal.

That's the Good News of the Gospel. There is no way to please God in and of ourselves. We cannot earn or work our way to heaven. We cannot do enough of anything to earn His favor in salvation, and we do not have to! He provided the way. He sacrificed His own Son to pay for our sins and to gain our salvation. He loves us so much, that He is not willing that any should perish. His Word tells us, "For God so loved the world, that He gave His only begotten Son, that whosoever believeth in Him should not perish, but have everlasting life" (John 3:16). Remember that straight-and-narrow way we spoke of? This is it. Ask Jesus to come into your heart! Romans 10:8–9 tells us that if we confess with our mouths the Lord Jesus and believe in our hearts that God raised Him from the dead, we will be saved. It says, "For with the heart man believeth unto righteousness and with the mouth confession is made unto salvation."

We are all on our way to the tank right now. Jesus said, "I am the way, the truth, and the life: no man cometh unto the Father, but by me." The only time you can make your deal is now, before you get in His presence. You will not be allowed to make a pitch after you die. There will be no time to make an impressive presentation. Your eternal destiny is decided in the here and now, as you walk through the hall of your life.

The Bible is full of people who ended up dismissed at the end of the show, their presentations notwithstanding. Once, a rich young man came to Jesus, thinking he had his dynamite presentation set and his facts mastered and at hand. (See Mark 10:17–27.) He called Jesus "Good Master," a title pregnant with meaning. Jesus makes sure that he knows that the title he has just assigned Him is one only God can claim, as only God is truly good. The young man does not alter what he has said. He asks Jesus what he must do to inherit eternal life. Jesus decided to give him a more in-depth examination and did not immediately tell him about believing and following.

This happens on *Shark Tank* sometimes too. You listen to Kevin or Robert and you hear the words coming, "I'm going to make you an offer." Instead, they draw the person out and give some insight and counsel. They appear to be ready to get involved as they express a favorable opinion of the contestant. Then, they opt out.

So Jesus tells the young ruler that he must obey the commandments. "Which ones?" he asks. Jesus chooses to use the Ten Commandments. He drops the first four that have to do with our vertical relationship with God—since the young man has already given him that by calling Him "good"—and He moves to our horizontal relationships, the ones having to do with our relationships with others. The young man, brought up by Orthodox parents, knows these, has memorized them and has no problem affirming that he has kept these. In one Gospel account, it is recorded that when Jesus saw this He "loved him" (Mark 10:21). He was a bright, sincere young man, a solid prospect to follow Jesus. It looks like he is going to get a deal and leave the tank happy.

But Jesus has been precise in His language here, and He has done something many miss in a light reading of the passage. He has left out the commandment, "Thou shalt not covet." He is putting His finger on that one in the heart of this man, telling him to go and to sell all that he has and to give the proceeds to the poor. He deals with the one weakness in the young man's presentation. It's his "lack of sales." It is his poor performance the last quarter. It is the factor that will lead to an "I'm out."

This story is not here for a blanket application, so relax. God is not telling all of us that we must sell all that we have and give it away. He is telling us to get rid of whatever it is that is keeping us from surrendering wholly to Him and to His will for our lives. For the Rich Young Ruler, it is his great lust for material things. It was his desire to accumulate and to be wealthy. He has a divided heart. He ends up walking the long walk back down the corridor without sealing a deal. His presentation failed.

Often *Shark Tank* contestants, fresh from an encounter with the Sharks, will give an exit interview.

They frequently will lament that they were not ready to give up that much of their business as some Shark wanted a higher percentage of their company than they were prepared to give. The Rich Young Ruler's exit interview? He would have said something like, "I wasn't ready to give up that much of my company (life) to follow Jesus and to seal the deal." I believe he ended up like other contestants on the show, who later wondered, "What in the world was I thinking? I should have made the deal!" I am sure the young man has regretted his turning away from the Son of God many times.

But he, like the contestants, and like people in real life, set up false constructs as his personal standards to live and die by. Many of us do just that, just as many contestants on the show walk in and think they will wow, impress, and conquer, only to find out that they have been operating from a false set of principles and values. They were not ready for the questions, basic though they are.

I said the Bible is full of people, or contestants in the business of life, making their presentations and finding out that in the real world of absolutes with God, they are sorely lacking. One is a rich man who had been blessed with abundance. One year, for whatever reason, God gives him a bounty so large that it changes his life. (See Luke 12:16–21.)

He is forced to alter his plans. He is thinking, "More is good." He gets greedy and covetous too, just like our previous fellow. He is like many of the contestants on *Shark Tank*. I often marvel when they are offered a deal that is obviously very favorable to them. They are told by Lori or another Shark, "I will make you a millionaire. I will make you rich. Let's make a lot of money together!" But, against all that is sane or right, they hold out for more, or worse—they come back with a stingy offer sure to offend. They hold on to their company share or some high stake in it, and greedily ask for more! In many cases, we in the audience can tell the Shark was reluctant to do the deal but decided to have mercy and give the person presenting a chance. It is almost an act of charity for them to even get involved. You almost breathe a sigh of relief that the person will get something. But then, they make a ridiculous counter offer that shows they missed the generosity of their would-be benefactor completely. Often, the other Sharks will say a surprised, "Whoa ho!" in unison. One may point out that the presenter is making a big mistake, right before the ominous words inevitably come, "I'm out."

So it is with the rich man as his fields are blessed by God with super abundance. Does he take it thankfully? Does he humbly show gratitude and turn and bless others as God would have him to do? No! He looks around as though he has really done something, as if he is so special, and says to himself, "I'll tear down my old barns and build bigger ones to hold all of this." He is selfish. He is blind. The Bible tells us that God calls him a fool and takes his life that night. He's out, literally! Kevin O'Leary likes to tell people on the show, "You're dead to me! Get out!" God did just that with that rich man.

Another rich man in the Bible, in Luke 16:19 (are you picking up on a common theme there?), makes his entrance to the Shark Tank decked out in fine clothes of purple and fine linen (perhaps from FUBU?). He is wealthy. He literally lives in a gated community and enjoys the best things life has to offer every day. Shark Kevin O'Leary has revealed on the show that he has a certain fine wine or liquor at a certain time of the day, then another vintage of some sort, and then a last one before retiring. He shows a knowledge of fine foods, exotic foods, and can obviously have anything he wants. He is like the Rich Man in Jesus's story. He could be on the show as a billionaire Shark. He might even be, as Kevin, nicknamed "Mr. Wonderful." The title is a fictitious one as Kevin is just the opposite.

But Jesus's "Mr. Wonderful" would not invest! You see, he has that opportunity every day but does not take advantage of it. He has a beggar at his gate named Lazarus. Lazarus is there every day, making his pitch to him, as he is weak, sick, covered with sores and with rags. His life and world are very different from the one the rich man lives in. Lazarus just has the hope of getting some crumbs from the rich man's table. He dumpster dives hoping for leftovers.

But it is not Lazarus making the presentation here, is it? It is the rich man in his purple suit. Thyatiran shell fish were harvested and boiled to obtain a Tyrean purple dye, one so expensive that only the very wealthy or people of royalty could afford. He would be one of the rude contestants on the show, coming in with all of his wealth and power. He would be insulting, conceited, and proud. On *Shark Tank* there have been some heated squabbles as an already successful contestant comes in and tries to chop down one of the Sharks. Some of these may even rival a Shark in wealth. The Sharks do not take kindly to such.

There are people living their lives just as pompously. They do not fear God, they believe they are responsible for their wealth, for their achievements and for their position in life. Obviously, they think, their own brilliance has taken them to the top. They worked hard, learned the system, and succeeded. They are special. They don't need God. They do not defer to God. They take credit for their success (The Bible tells us that God is the One with the power to grant wealth.). They look down at those "laid by the gate" as such people are obviously inferior. So, as this rich man, they do not share or lend a hand to help others. They reek of ingratitude.

Such pompous people do not get a deal on *Shark Tank*, and they fare no better in real life either. The Bible tells us that God resists the proud and that the proud in heart are an abomination to Him. Jesus made a famous pronouncement on the rich, saying that it is easier for a camel to go through the eye of a needle than for a rich man to enter His kingdom (Mark 10:25). That would seem to make it impossible, but Jesus quickly added that His Father could do the impossible. He was saying in effect that it almost takes a miracle with some of these arrogant people.

The man in the purple clothes dies and goes to hell. He suffers torment, he begs for a drop of water from the beggar Lazarus's fingertip, and he shows he now understands. He knows his presentation did not make it with God. He did not believe what God had written in His Word. What God expected was well known, but he rejected it. God operates from absolutes and one of those absolutes is that we trust His Son and give Him our lives. We acknowledge that we need Him. We come to Him humbly, willing to do anything He says to win His favor and to get His partnership.

As noted, you can live your life entirely from a false construct. You can put together an impressive presentation with a portfolio, a" knock your socks" off one—one that you will feel comfortable enough to die with. And just as this man did, shockingly, you will find yourself totally rejected and unsuccessful in your appeal.

Jesus told of two men who went up to the temple to pray (Luke 18:10). They had a very different way of presenting themselves to God. The first, a religious leader known as a Pharisee, looked up proudly and boasted of all of his good works, all he had done—tithing, all of it. The second would not even raise his head, he was so humble. He came in and begged, "God be merciful to me a sinner." Jesus said it was the second man who got a deal with God! He ended up justified. The Pharisee put his life out there in his presentation and found he had missed the point of it all.

CHAPTER 2

THE MOST IMPORTANT QUESTIONS ARE BASICALLY THE SAME

BUSINESS IS SO much like life. It is life, and the basic questions of life come up again and again on *Shark Tank*. If you have watched the show you know that the Sharks want to know pretty quickly and routinely, "What do you value your business at? What are your sales? Over what period have you enjoyed that success?" They will want to know upfront what you are asking for and usually will follow quickly with, "What are you going to do with the money? What will you do if we give you what you want? Are you willing to compromise, meet half way, or alter your original proposal?"

So let's apply it. You are in business right now. You are in the business of building a life. It may include a family with a mate, offspring, and the people who brought you up. It probably includes a circle of friends and more family; a job, hobbies, interests, and passions. How much do you value it? Is it really worth it? What do you want? On what basis do you reply?

On *Shark Tank* people are constantly coming in with vastly overvalued businesses. The Sharks, the investors, are not just operating by opinions and feelings, though Lori frequently enjoins the pitchman to "follow your heart." They operate by cold hard realities, the verities of the business world.

In fact, that vexed me when I first began to watch the shows. I was amazed at how different the Sharks were from me. Their perceptions of companies, people, and who was worthy and who was not worthy to be invested in were far different than mine. Their thinking was clearly not my thinking. They were obviously operating from a different paradigm than mine. Of course, my perspective as a people person, as an extrovert, as a pastor, as someone who loves people and wants to see people encouraged, redeemed, and invested in, my approach was skewed toward investing in everyone! I was even angry at times when the Sharks curtly condemned some poor guy and sent him into oblivion! And even as I began to alter my thinking with that in mind, even as I tried to look at this more objectively from a business perspective, I was constantly at odds with the investors. I would guess which people they would partner with and was wrong about 50 percent of the time. I would try to judge from the beginning of the pitch, who would get an investment and from whom. I was invariably wrong most of the time.

Why? Because their absolutes guided them—their MBA absolutes, their "lessons learned in the world of business" absolutes! Kevin O'Leary processed his absolutes by asking, "What is proprietary about this? What did they have that no one else had? What could he license from what they had patented? And of course, how could he make money?" Mark Cuban, who seems to have the most business education, wanted to know if they had followed the well-worn path of business to a point where they were a business and not just a few finished products made in their garage. Lori, looks for three things: 1) Is the product something people need and want? 2) Will it be of interest to a broad audience? 3) Can it be made affordably?

For all it is, how long had they been in business, what were their overall sales? What were their most recent sales? And what was affecting their sales? Woe to those who are unprepared to answer these questions with numbers and facts! And most of the time, the subjective evaluations placed on the businesses by the business pitchmen themselves are way overinflated. Deals could still be achieved but at much lower evaluations.

So back to your life. How long have you been at this? Your life is your business. For the Sharks, "how long" indicates whether a business is paying off and if it is growing. Life is the same. As in business, when we are younger, we may be just finding our way. There may be a learning curve, but the longer we have been at any business, including living our lives, the more profitable it should be. It is not unlike a twelve-year-old boy who told his teacher he was worried. "Why?" asked the teacher. "Because I don't know what I want to do with my life. I don't know who I want to be." The teacher replied, "You have nothing to worry about. That is a common concern when you are twelve. Now if you are still asking and don't know by the time you are fifty, then your life will have been a failure."

So how long have you been in business? What is your life worth today? Where are you investing your time, your passion, your energy? Do you have an ever larger circle of people to whom you really matter, who derive a part of their own significance and value from their acquaintance and friendship with you? Are you investing in others, adding value to others? Are you operating with the radical principles of Jesus as your guide? When you get up in the morning, what is most important to you as you go out into your day? Making money? Making a name? Or making a difference?

You see, we could all use a type of *Shark Tank*. Friends and acquaintances might never push us with the hard questions and the stark realities. We might not have anyone in our circle to tell us, "Let me do you a favor. This part of your life (your business) is going nowhere! Stop! End the madness!" as Kevin likes to put it. "Put your talent and passion into something else. This is a dead end!" We may never have anyone in our lives operating from absolute rules and values to tell us, "Something in your life (business) just does not add up. The numbers don't add up, you are going in too many directions."

There are people you can pay to advise you on what to do with your portfolio. You can hire a life coach to help you attain certain goals. There may be some friends you can go to for the hard truth and you may even find some help from the critics in your life. The critics truly are the guardians of our souls, and there really is a grain of truth in every criticism.

Our lives are too important and too valuable to waste. They are too brief to squander. As an older friend of mine told me recently, we all have an expiration date. We need to make the most of it. We need to learn the absolutes—the answers to the basic questions—from the best possible source. Even the people whom the Sharks scold and send packing learn from the process and the direction and corrections put forth. We do not want to end up at the end of the show (the close of our lives) bewildered with a very different summation of our business (our lives) than the one we believed in.

The Shark contestants often appear shocked when the little world they constructed, when what they thought was solid, is ripped to shreds. The cameras on the show love to catch the "deer in the headlights" look. In fact, that happens so frequently that I thought they might be scripting it, that they might even be holding rehearsals. They claim they are not. And neither are you! Your life is not a rehearsal. It is real! If you are operating off a false set of values and guides, you need to know now! You need the right answers to the most important questions of all—the eternal questions.

The best possible source of all to answer the basic life's questions is the Word of God. The Bible as someone put it, is the B-I-B-L-E: Basic Instruction Before Leaving Earth. God made us. God knows us. God loves us. God is absolutely passionate about you. If He had a refrigerator, your picture would be on it. Your phone number would be written on a scrap of paper and in His wallet, if He carried one. He has a plan for your life, a purpose for your life, and He delights in being with you and about you. His Word is truly a lamp unto our feet and a light unto our path. He truly does provide instruction, guidance, and leading. What is your life worth? It cost Him His Son on the cross to redeem you. Of what value are you today? You are an integral part of what He wants to do in your sphere of influence. Every breath you take, every precious moment He grants you gives value, inestimable value, to your life (business). You are living for and investing in your eternity every day! It's your life! Value it highly, and set its evaluation skyward! He wants to invest in you to the fullest!

So the questions are basic? How about, "How much are you asking for?" Isn't that a most basic question? It is the last item on the pitch person's opening statement. They will say something like, "Today I am asking for $250,000 for 20 percent of my company." The Sharks can be seen scribbling furiously and quickly computing that this person values their company at $1.25 million. Away we go!

Don't you know that a lot of thought goes into the company owners' computations on their value? In fact, most seem to be operating in another world than that of the Sharks. Almost all the evaluations are way to high and the Sharks will quickly point this out and tell them why. They will chop away at this as their time together goes on. I have watched enough now to know that entrepreneurs use all kinds of standards to come up with their figure and most are faulty standards. They will often claim they are hard workers with great passion. They just know they are going to do tremendously after they get a website, sales force, advertising campaign, cheaper source for manufacturing, and a Shark partner.

"What will you do if you get what you want?" The Sharks ask this of almost every pitchman. Some say they will hire a sales force. Some say they will build up inventory or perhaps build a plant. Others promise to get FDA approval or pursue a patent. Some say they have never taken a salary and will use some of what they get to pay themselves. (That answer is a big no-no and is shot down every time!) Sometimes an answer suffices. Sometimes it leads to another "I'm out" response from a Shark.

Have you ever asked yourself what you would do if you got what you wanted? What is it that you want? Is it big? Is it bold? Will it outlive you? Will it satisfy?

Or is it one of those "what we learn from history is that we never learn from history." conundrums? In other words, those who have gone on before us were pretty much just like us. They "wanted" just like we do, and like a river, they flowed down the paths of least resistance. Money, power, sex, possessions—all were wanted, acquired, and found wanting. People spent their lives trying to satisfy themselves with these things—things they thought they needed, things they thought would make them happy. That's right. People achieved the acquisition of most of the things we want. And guess what? Like *Shark Tank* participants, we ended up pouring our resources (lives) into areas that do not bring a return. It's too bad we do not have to explain to an expert what we would do if we got what they wanted. It would save us a lot of grief.

And yet, that same Bible I mentioned earlier, can guide us to make the wise decision on what we want and what we will do when we get it. For example, on the matter of our desire to have things, to acquire things, and to get more things, Jesus said, "Take heed of covetousness: for a man's life consisteth not in the abundance of the things which he possesseth" (Luke 12:15). So true! Things do not make a life. Having a lot does not make one successful, happy, and fulfilled.

Jesus also said in Matthew 6:24, "No man can serve two masters; for either he will hate the one, and love the other; or else he will hold to the one and despise the other. Ye cannot serve God and mammon." Mammon is money and material possessions. Money makes a very poor master. Wealth is never secure and cannot be relied on. The Bible tells us in 1 Timothy 6:17 in the training of a young minister, that he is to "charge them that are rich in this world, that they be not highminded, nor trust in uncertain riches, but in the living God, who giveth us richly all things to enjoy." The wisest man who ever lived, imbued with wisdom from God, wrote in Proverbs 23:5, "Wilt thou set thine eyes upon that which is not? for riches certainly make wings for themselves, and fly away as an eagle toward heaven."

After asking what will be done with the money, the Sharks often admonish the entrepreneur in front of them, "No, no, no! Before you build up inventory you need sales!" Kevin may get downright insulting and harsh, telling them if they don't get a patent that one of the big boys in the same business will copy them and crush them "like the cockroach they are." That is offensive, but look beyond the various coarse words and see that these savvy millionaires are pointing out the weakness of the contestant's plan and telling them, "That's not a wise way to use our investment in you."

You want a return on your life. You don't want to give all your passion, time, energy, sweat, and tears to something, only to get it and find it empty. What are you going to do when you get what you want? Make sure it stands the test of eternity. Make sure it will bring true contentment. Make sure it is legacy worthy.

CHAPTER 3

THE ASK

YOU CAN IMAGINE that a lot of thought and planning goes into "the ask." Sometimes, in the preshow interviews where a contestant is interviewed in their own setting, you can see that they are asking for something that will set them free. As they tell their story, they introduce their business and tell of their needs. Some want to get enough to pay off their parents, families, or trust investors. One contestant had mortgaged everything and needed a certain amount or he was going to lose it all—business, home, the works. "If I don't get what I'm asking for, I don't know what I'll do. I have to get it." That is the lament of many.

The Sharks have shown a willingness to invest a great deal of money, and million-dollar deals have been made. Again, because their world is a whole different world and because they operate from a whole other set of parameters, sometimes this can seem puzzling to us novices. I've seen deals that I thought were solid gold for a low price. For a pittance, a Shark could have a huge portion of some enterprise with very low risk, which could become something I thought would be profitable. These deals often involved people for whom help from a Shark might have been nice. But being nice is not the goal! The Sharks turned them down, having seen something I did not see. Or maybe they just did not feel generous that day!

And then, there are the proposals that seem, to me, to be tailor-made to be rejected, dismissed, and done so with prejudice. Suddenly, a couple of the Sharks eagerly begin a bidding war, trying to partner with the contestant. Sometimes even the pitchman, as sold out on their business as they are, seems surprised to have all of that action. It is, to put it in real shark vernacular, a "feeding frenzy." Two Sharks may come together and share an offer. They may even do this to beat out another Shark. Whatever is being asked is granted. Sometimes, because of the competition, it is even increased.

So what are you asking for? What do you want?

Did you know that there is a fierce competition for you? As C. S. Lewis, the Catholic theologian once said, every day, God and Satan contest for every square inch of this world. You are the prize! God loves you so much, so intensely, and so passionately! He gave the ultimate to make the deal for your soul—His only begotten Son. He purchased your right to heaven and a glorious eternal existence.

He outbid everyone else. He offered you far more than you imagined.

The apostle Paul wrote most of the New Testament. He wrote in one of his church letters, in Ephesians 2:4, "But God, who is rich in mercy, for his great love wherewith he loved us." That's what it is! It is a great love, the greatest of all.

In another letter, which also became a book, the Book of Galatians, chapter 2, verse 20, he writes three words that are astounding and among my most favorite in the Scriptures. He wrote, "…and the life which I now live in the flesh, I live by the faith of the Son of God, *who loved me,* and gave Himself for me" (emphasis added). "Who loved me"—what an astounding thought!

How do we determine the value of something, of anything" Let's say you are going to sell your house or your car. What will you ask for it? You will probably look at Kelly Blue Book to see what value it estimates for the car. You may look in the classified ads to see what either should sell for. You may get an appraisal on the house. These tools will help you determine what to ask.

On *Shark Tank*, the entrepreneurs, as noted, often value capriciously. They may overevaluate based on projected sales, a round of fund raising, or on what they have invested so far. The Sharks quickly shoot down most of these evaluations.

But again, how do we determine the value of

anything? What is any business or product really worth?

It is simple. It is worth what someone is willing to pay for it! A Shark contestant may think his business is worth $500,000. However, he may end up partnering in a deal that says it is worth $300,000. So the value is determined by what Lori or Barbara is willing to pay. At the end of the day, the same is true of anything we sell. It is worth only what we can get for it.

God gave His precious Son for you!

And He did not stop there! He came to give us an abundant life! He came to give us a life worth living, a life where every day is an adventure, complete with meaning, purpose, and fulfillment. He saves us from hell, and because of His great love, He gives us a wonderful life!

What are you asking for? Life is brief. The Bible likens our days to a tale that is told about grass growing in the morning and then being cut down in the evening. It likens our years here as flowers that flourish and then the wind passes over and we are gone. (See Psalm 103:15–26.) When asked what the biggest surprise of his life had been, Evangelist Billy Graham replied, "The greatest surprise in life to me is its brevity." This moment is all we really have. It is a gift, a present, which is, we might say, a present. Our days are numbered.

In the Tank, the decisions must be made quickly. At some point, a Shark, usually Kevin or Robert, will sum up the offers that have been made. They will give the numbers, the equity required, and tell the contestant,

"You have to make up your mind now. Do you accept an offer?" This is it! This is the big moment. What they decide is destiny altering.

So, what are you asking for? Go big! Ask for eternal life! Ask for the joy! Ask for the partnership that will get you into the kingdom of God and all that He is doing! Ask for His salvation and accept the offer of His love. You need never look back. His offer is above all offers, and it will enrich you now and forever. You can have a deal, and, in the end, He is providing all of the equity.

CHAPTER 4

SOME THINGS YOU THOUGHT MATTERED, DON'T!

OFTEN SEE CONTESTANTS come in who make exhaustive, extensive defenses of their negotiating position and have come to recognize certain familiar refrains.

Usually these come when they realize that they have nothing else tangible to offer. They make an emotional appeal hoping to sway a Shark when their numbers, sales, assets, and business plan do not seem to be impressive enough to gain a partner.

For example, many will say, "I am passionate about this. I work harder than anybody. I will get this done. I eat and sleep my business. I am tenacious. I don't quit."

Mark Cuban will usually shoot that down in a hurry! He will point out that nearly everyone who comes into the tank feels the same way and that it does not affect the bottom line. Lots of people work very hard, and Mark does not doubt the validity of their statement. It's just inconsequential to the Sharks' decision-making process.

Some will tell how they had a great trade show with lots of interest. They may offer that a big box store picked them up and carried their product in X amount of stores for a while. The Sharks will press on how many orders, were there reorders, and why not. One poor lady said it was doing fine until they put it in the back of the stores. Sales tanked. The Sharks explained that no store puts hot items in the back of the store. It went back there because it was getting nowhere.

Others will seek to impress by telling the Sharks that they have invested a lot of money. They peg dollar amounts that are often quite high. The Sharks will shake their heads, Kevin will say, "Stop the madness!" and most will offer the advice to stop now, cut your losses, and get out. It is sad to see someone who has invested all their money, mortgaged their home, borrowed from friends and family, leave the tank with no deal and a dire summation of his prospects of ever making it.

We may be, and probably are, unconsciously putting together something similar for our final presentation. We often construct the best possible case we can for why we should be accepted by God. We work very hard at it, at living a good life—at being kind to the old and very young, and at being a loving and generous person. By our own standards we are doing well. As we watch the news at night and interact with other people, we see people living immoral, tawdry, and sinful lives, and we judge that we are doing a lot better than they are and we may even think we are doing better than most.

A lot of well-meaning people believe they will come to no harm before God, that they will leave the tank with a deal based on their own set of standards and ideas of what will sway God to partner with them. After all, they have really worked hard! Sadly, they will be surprised and disappointed when they pass from this life.

God is not looking for hard workers. He is not looking for "good" people. He is not deciding on whether to partner with you or not, based upon your performance. No construct that you can make will gain His investment in you.

You see, He has already concluded that "all have sinned and come short of the glory of God" (Rom. 3:23). He has already declared, "There is none righteous, no not one" (Rom. 3:10). He, like the Sharks, has His own standard to judge by. It is the perfect standard of His perfect, sinless Son, Jesus Christ. He will, like the Sharks, reject any and all self-constructed standard or standards we may come up with. Like those on the show, He will use only His own to judge by.

I read a story years ago of a chaplain in Tennessee. He had to go to Nashville and decided to take his young son with him. They spent the night in a motel.

The next day they went over to a diner for breakfast. The place was busy so they ended up sitting on the stools at a big counter. A waitress took their order and while they waited for their food a young man came in and sat on a stool next to the father. When their food came, the father and son prayed together over their meal. When they finished, the man said, "That's nice!" The father asked, "Oh, that we prayed? Are you a Christian too?" "No," said the man, "I was talking about the fact that you and your son are close, praying, having breakfast. That's nice. And no, I'm not a Christian."

Well, the chaplain asked him if he would like to know more about God. He quoted John 3:16: "For God so loved the world that He gave His only begotten Son, that whosoever believeth in Him should not perish but have everlasting life." He said, "You would like to have your sins forgiven and have everlasting life, wouldn't you?" The young guy replied, "I appreciate what you're saying but I will be fine. I've always lived my life by this creed: 'A life well spent knows no loss.' I believe that when I die, God will look at my life, see that I did the best I know how, and I will suffer no loss."

Well, the chaplain tried, without wanting to be too pushy to explain that we can't make it up, we have to accept the Bible, but he got nowhere. They ended their conversation on friendly terms and ate their food.

As they were leaving, they both ended up at the register. The young man stuck out his hand and said, "Nice to meet you." The chaplain replied, "It was nice to meet you. I really like you. Please remember what

I told you. God loves you." He then quoted John 3:16 again. And the reply was, "And you remember what I told you; "A life well spent knows no loss." He said good-bye and left.

Many do just that. Many make up their own standard. To him it made perfect sense that if he just lived his life well, he would not suffer hell and eternity in torment. We cannot do that. God has spoken in His Word. He has His standard and it is His perfect Son. None of us can live up to that standard.

The good news—that's what the word *gospel* means— is that we don't have to. He paid the price, He justifies by faith in the finished work of Jesus. We just have to ask Him to come into our heart and save us. If we will go by His standard, we will get the partnership, and the best of all partnerships. We won't leave the tank empty handed!

CHAPTER 5

THERE IS A MR. WONDERFUL, BUT HIS NAME IS NOT KEVIN

S THE SEASONS go by, the business tycoons take on a certain persona and we get to know them. Their personal lives are fodder for the media. Robert Herjevic, for example, has shown himself to be a really decent guy. He especially has a soft spot for immigrants and those who, like himself and his parents, came here with nothing more than a dream. He will often offer a deal when no one else will. He gets a little testy when someone wants to entertain more offers and may quit in a pique with a quick, "I'm out." We learned from various media outlets that his marriage failed over the last couple of seasons and it took a toil on him. He says his pastor really helped him (When's the last time you heard that from someone in primetime?) and that his stint on *Dancing With the Stars* has been so physically demanding that it has been therapeutic for him.

The Shark's personalities and their personal stories come out as they talk to those who would like to partner with them. Their peculiar little idiosyncrasies do too. None has developed a persona or character more than Kevin O'Leary, who is facetiously called "Mr. Wonderful."

Contestants now address him as Mr. Wonderful. His vanity license plates have "Mr. Wonderful" on them. He often jests that his deal is the best because, after all, he is Mr. Wonderful. How could he not be helping an investor?

However, he is doing anything but! His deals are incredibly one-sided. He almost always asks for royalties in perpetuity, even as the other Sharks attack him for his greed. He is rough and tough on all contestants. None are spared his wrath, ridicule, sarcasm, and cruel ways of stripping someone down to nothing but "the cockroach that you are." Men, women, young, old—none are spared from his torrent of abuse. He is anything but "wonderful."

In all fairness, much of that is an act and he has shown himself at times to be a decent guy. He likes to portray himself as, well, a vicious Shark, what else? He likes to be the bad guy with the hard questions. He will say over and over again, "How can I make money? Tell me where the money is! All I care about is the money!" He knows how he is being perceived. He will even get into sharp exchanges with the other Sharks. Mr. Wonderful, he is not!

But, there is a Mr. Wonderful and his name is not Kevin O'Leary! His name is actually Wonderful, or at least one of them is. In the Old Testament, the Bible says of Jesus in a prophecy in Isaiah 9:6, "For unto us a child is born, unto us a son is given: and the government shall be upon his shoulder: and his name shall be called, Wonderful, Counselor, the mighty God, the everlasting Father, the Prince of Peace." That prophecy was given over seven hundred years before He was born.

And, wonderful He is! Just, kind, loving, sacrificing, humble, meek, strong, controlled, powerful, perfect in integrity—He is all that and more! He is wonderful! There is nothing and no one like Him!

When you make a deal with God, you will not be taken advantage of. You will be taking advantage of His great love for you. He wants to give you forgiveness. He wants to give you redemption. He wants to give you forgiveness of sins. He wants to give you eternity in a perfectly wonderful body in a perfectly wonderful place doing perfectly wonderful things.

He is pro-you! He is not trying to "take you," cheat you, gain advantage of you, use you, or profit from you. As much as you have nothing to offer Him, He has everything to offer you. He is Mr. Wonderful beyond imagination. He loves you.

Mr. Wonderful (Kevin) has power over the people who enter into the Tank. It is not absolute. One of the other Sharks may make a deal with someone he has rejected. They frequently disagree with him, rebuke him, and try to build up people he has torn down and destroyed with his tongue. They do this even when they are not going to seek a deal. But at times, he is the last Shark left to make a deal as the others have bowed out. For a contestant, that is a fearful place to be, totally at his mercy. He may offer an insulting deal, he may further excoriate the person, or he may just contemptuously dismiss them as the incompetent, clueless buffoons he believes them to be. He knows he has the power, he is in control, and he enjoys it.

There are only two competitors seeking an agreement with you. The loving God I have described is one. There is another. The Bible teaches that one of God's own special cherubim—an angel—fell, as he in pride, thought he could rise up and be God's equal. In the Bible, he is called Lucifer, Satan, the devil, Beelzebub, the serpent, and several more unsavory names. He knows what his end will be as God has already told in His Word that he will be cast into a lake of fire prepared for him and his fallen angels. He will spend eternity there. His desire then is to take as many people as he can with him. God has heaven for human beings who accept His offer of salvation in Christ, and hell for Satan and the fallen angels. He has no place in heaven for those who reject His Son, so they will also spend eternity in hell.

When Kevin O'Leary as Mr. Wonderful, gets into competition with the other Sharks for an individual, he is motivated by his desire to make a deal that he will profit from, usually at the contestant's expense. Sometimes it will be down to him and one other Shark. This is what the bidding war going on for you is like; two bidders going head-to-head. When the real Mr. Wonderful, our God, fights for your soul, He has already paid a tremendous cost and it is all to your benefit. He wants you to come and be saved. He does not want to lose you. He does not want you to suffer eternal separation and damnation. You have never met anyone so wonderful—one who has more concern for your well-being, who loves you more, and who will give you more—as God. He will do this all through Jesus Christ.

Satan on the other hand has nothing. He offers nothing but pain, ruin, and death. He lies and deceives. And, like Kevin, he will want royalties forever. The payments, at your expense, will never end. He wants far more from you than you can afford.

On *Shark Tank*, contestants often see just how terrible Mr. Wonderful's offers are. They will spurn him and leave the Tank with other Sharks commending them for refusing the deal. Mark Cuban will call out, "Good for you!" You don't want to do that with God, our Mr. Wonderful. But you certainly want to walk out on what Satan is offering, and the sooner the better. Take Christ up on His offer right now!

CHAPTER 6

DON'T LOSE THE OFFER! IT'S A GREAT ONE!

A S NOTED, ONE contestant after another comes in with equity values that are more than unreasonable. They might ask for $200,000 for 5 percent of their equity (he is saying his business is worth $4 million), or $500,000 for 20 percent (he is saying his business is worth $2.5 million.) The Sharks quickly do their computations and will usually ask pretty quickly, "Why do you think you are worth that?"

Why indeed? So off they go in defense of their "ask" and their value. They cite their sales, prospects, current locations for sales (usually the Internet), inventory, and projections. Almost all who settle, end up with far less in the value of their company and give up far more equity than they had intended.

Well, for your business—your life, that is—God will partner with you but He will want all of your equity. He wants all of you! He wants you to sell out to Him. He wants you to surrender all to Him and to His control. He wants to manage your company, He wants to make the plans, and He wants to lead, guide, direct, and control.

I often see bumper stickers that say, "God is my copilot." God is not your "co-" anything! He is the sovereign God of the universe. He formed you, He made you, and He brought you to life. He wants to take over, but it is not a hostile takeover. He wants to run your life, but He will not ruin your life. He loves you and will always work everything in your life out for your good!

Sometimes the Sharks will offer to buy someone out completely. Kevin (Mr. Wonderful Kevin) was particularly harsh on one poor entrepreneur, offering him a million dollars for his business and then telling him he never wanted to see him again. He wanted him out. He insulted him and told him he was worthless and that he would take the company and do something with it, without him. The guy was crushed.

God wants you, totally, for your own good! God wants you completely, for what's best for you! Jesus said, "I have come that they might have life and that they might have it more abundantly" (John 10:10). He brings us joy, peace, contentment, and fulfillment. When we sell out to Him, completely, He then does marvelous things in us and through us.

So, surrender all your equity to Him. He will give

you eternal life in heaven. He will give you a new body, perfect health, and a wondrous place to live for all eternity. He will so order your life that it will matter, it will count, it will be an adventure and it will have a legacy that was worth living.

Sometimes the Sharks and the audience get it. An offer has been made, an overly generous offer, and the contestant is hesitating, mulling it over. Often this occurs after four Sharks have opted out, leaving only one. The four have made a strong case as to why they will not make an offer and there is surprise that one of the Sharks is. Mr. Wonderful will usually opine, "Are you crazy?" Mark Cuban will smile broadly and tell the pitchman, "You better take it now!" The idea is that this Shark will come to his senses and retract it.

Sometimes the contestant will ask to make a phone call. Sometimes, as noted, they will counter with something far different. All the Sharks will moan loudly as they see the foolishness of this person, toying with a generous and merciful offer, one that should be accepted immediately. The phone call request will be turned down as the Shark making the offer feels the offer he has made is so obviously good and so generous that this person must make the decision on the spot or lose it forever. The counteroffer is also turned down. The Shark believes his or her offer is already more than enough. It is final.

The offer God has made us is just like that. Don't lose the offer! Take it now. Don't mull it over, don't sleep on it, and don't make a phone call. Don't bargain with a counteroffer. His offer is so great, and obviously

45

so, that you just need to accept it. What you do with the offer of salvation, by faith in Jesus Christ, the resurrected Son of God, will determine where you spend eternity. When you are done with the offer, when your life is over, there will never be a redo. There will never be another opportunity. *Shark Tank* has had one returning contestant that I know of. After we die, we will never have another chance to receive Christ. There will be no returning.

If you would like to accept God's generous offer to you for your business—that is, your life—please do so now. Pray this prayer and accept Christ:

> *Dear Lord Jesus, I give myself to You. Please forgive me for my sins. Please come into my heart and save me. I give You my life, my heart, and my soul. Save me. In Jesus name, amen.*

You have a deal! If someone got a deal like this on *Shark Tank*, we would all be watching in disbelief. It would mean that some Shark or, perhaps more in partnership, and had given their all to go in with us. It would mean that they saw such value in having us in their life, that they were willing to go to the greatest extremes to make it happen. That is what you just got! Your Father in heaven gave His all to get you, because He wants to be with you. He loves you. He really is Mr. Wonderful.

Congratulations! If you were on the show, you would be one of those exulting, shouting, and telling the cameras, "I got just the deal I wanted with the Shark I wanted." Such entrepreneurs walk off with great joy at the prospects ahead. You can do that too. You just gained more than you can imagine! God bless you!

EPILOGUE

MARK BURNETT'S STRING of successes shows no
sign of ending! He has *The Voice, The Appren-
tice, Are You Smarter Than a Fifth Grader?,
Survivor, Rock Star, The Bible,* and many more. At the
time of this writing, a *Shark Tank* spinoff, *Beyond the
Tank,* was scheduled to debut. It will follow the Sharks
with those they have invested in and show how they
fare off the show and away from the happy deals.

Some of those who appear on *Beyond the Tank* end
up not doing so well. That will never happen to you.
Once you trust Christ, you will never need to look
back. Your story will have the most joyful of endings,
and an eternal, bright, new beginning. You will never
lose anything, now or in eternity.

I'd like to know how you fare after reading this
book. If you come to know the Lord, if you have what
Billy Graham calls, "a moment of decision," please
e-mail, write, or message me. I will share in your joy
and in the moment when someday, we pass through

the long corridor and into the presence of a loving and accepting God.

Best wishes my friend! God bless you!

E-MAIL: WILLIAMKHATFIELD@GMAIL.COM

FACEBOOK: WWW.FACEBOOK.COM/

WILLIAM.K.HATFIELD

ABOUT THE AUTHOR

WILLIAM HATFIELD HAS been married to Sharon for forty-two years. They have six children and thirteen grandchildren. He has pastored at the Charity Baptist Church, in Tulsa, OK, since 1979. He is a past chairman of the board at the Thornton YMCA, member of the International Fellowship of Christian Businessmen, and charter member of the American Association of Christian Counselors. He attended Eastern Michigan University and received his bachelor of arts in theology at Baptist Bible College. He graduated magna cum laude from the International Seminary with a master's degree in theology. His other books include, *A Heart for God*, *When God Empties You*, *The Distinctions Between the Kingdom of Heaven and the Kingdom of God*, and *Dynamics for Living*. Last year, he published his first e-book, *How to Coach Youth Soccer*, a book springing from over fifteen years of coaching on the pitch. He and Sharon reside in Tulsa, OK.